OTHER NATURE GIFTBOOKS BY EXLEY:
Country Lover's Notebook   Flowers a Celebration
Garden Lover's Quotations   Roses a Celebration
Flower Lover's Birthday Book   Illustrated Gardener's Notebook
Joy of Nature Address Book   Wonder of Flowers Address Book

Published simultaneously in 1993 by Exley Publications in Great
Britain, and Exley Giftbooks in the USA.
Second edition 1994.
Reprinted 1995.

EDITED BY HELEN EXLEY
Border illustrations by Juliette Clarke

Copyright © Helen Exley 1993.
ISBN 1-85015-428-7

Pictures and quotations selected by Helen Exley.
Designed by Pinpoint Design.
Picture research by P. A. Goldberg and J. Clift/Image Select, London.
Typeset by Delta, Watford.
Printed and bound by Grafo, S.A., Bilbao, Spain.

Exley Publications Ltd, 16 Chalk Hill, Watford, Herts WDl 4BN,
United Kingdom.
Exley Giftbooks, 232 Madison Avenue, Suite 1206, New York,
NY 10016, USA.
Picture credits: Archiv Fur Kunst: cover; Fine Art Photographic
Library: title page; Archiv Fur Kunst, Berlin: pages 34, 54;
Bridgeman Art Library, London and The Victoria and Albert
Museum: page 18; Bridgeman Art Library, London: pages 22, 44;
Bridgeman Art Library and Mass Gallery, London: page 51; Fine
Art Photographic Library: pages 6, 8, 12, 14, 21, 24, 26, 32, 36, 41,
56, 60.

NATURE
Lovers
A D D R E S S B O O K

EDITED BY HELEN EXLEY

NEW YORK • WATFORD, UK

A

I believe that a leaf of grass is no less than the
journey-work of the stars....

WALT WHITMAN (1819-1892)

[Nature] is the one place where miracles not only happen,
but happen all the time.

THOMAS WOLFE (1900-1938)

B

B

B

No two days are alike, not even two hours; neither were
there ever two leaves alike since the creation of the world.

JOHN CONSTABLE

C

*When I can be motionless long enough, there is no limit
I have ever reached to the revelations in an opening bud.*

VIDA D. SCUDDER

D

If you truly love Nature,
you will find beauty everywhere.
VINCENT VAN GOGH (1853-1890)

Happy are those who see beauty in modest spots
where others see nothing.

CAMILLE PISSARRO (1830-1903)

G

H

*Everything in nature invites us constantly to be
what we are.*

GRETEL EHRLICH

L

L

M

Nature does nothing uselessly.
ARISTOTLE

M

_____

_____

_____

_____

_____

_____

_____

_____

_____

_____

_____

P/Ç

_____

_____

_____

I go to Nature to be soothed and healed, and to have my senses put in tune once more.

JOHN BURROUGHS

P/Q

R

R

*Here is calm so deep, grasses cease waving... wonderful how
completely everything in wild nature fits into us....*

JOHN MUIR (1838-1914)

One touch of nature makes the whole world kin.

WILLIAM SHAKESPEARE (1564-1616)

Sympathy with nature is an evidence of perfect health.
You cannot perceive beauty but with a serene mind.

HENRY DAVID THOREAU (1817-1862)

Nothing which we can imagine about
Nature is incredible.

PLINY THE ELDER (23-79)

_____

_____

_____

_____

_____

_____

_____

_____

_____

_____

_____

_____

_____

U/V/W

_____

We look too much to museums. The sun coming up
in the morning is enough.

ROMARE BEARDEN

U/V/W

X/Y/Z

Nature is the greatest show on earth.

ANONYMOUS